The Welsh Presbyterian Mission in Sylhet, Bangladesh and Jaintia Hills, India

The Welsh Presbyterian Mission in Sylhet, Bangladesh and Jaintia Hills, India

Memoirs of the Lewis Family

Merilyn Lewis

John Roberts Theological College

&

Christian World Imprints

First Published in 2020 by

John Roberts Theological College
Mawklot, **Shillong-793009**
jrts.principal@gmail.com
www.johnrobertstheologicalseminary.co.in
Phone: 0364-2560364

&

Christian World Imprints
Christian Publishing & Books from India
C-3, Wazirpur Industrial Area
Delhi-110052
cwidelhi2017@gmail.com
www.ChristianWorldImprints.com
Phone: +91 11 41526079

ISBN: 978-93-5148-444-8

Cover Description:

Back Row: Mrs Roberts, Mrs Bannerjee, Mrs Dutta, My Mother
Front Row: Mr Ghose, Mr Dutta (Sylhet late1933)

Printed in India.

Dedicated to my parents

Watcyn Leslie Lewis 1903-1952
Winifred Betty Lewis 1910-2003
and to the many Indian colleagues who were part of their lives

CONTENTS

FOREWORD-I

The book is a narration by Marilyn Lewis of the experiences of her parents, Watcyn Leslie Lewis (1903-1952) and Winifred Betty Lewis (1910-2003), who worked as missionaries in Maulvibazaar (Bangladesh), Shangpung and Jowai (India) from 1933 to 1939. The narration is based on the memoirs (letters and diaries) left behind by her parents and also the life story which was dictated by Winifred to Marilyn. As per the narration, the couple spent around three years in Maulvibazaar, six months in Shangpung, and for two and a half years in Jowai. Though the tenure at each station was short, yet one can feel the excitement and enthusiasm of the couple while doing mission despite the fact that it was a period of tension with the World War II looming over the minds and thoughts of those in Europe. Readers with a keen eye for details and researchers will find this book interesting as some of the information are worth pondering. This narration can also be considered to be a unique as it connects Maulvibazaar in Bangladesh to Shangpung in India.

May we all be blessed through this book.

Rev. Dr. B. J. Syiemlieh
Principal
John Roberts Theological College
Shillong

FOREWORD-II

The book is an album in words, documenting the service of two dedicated souls who responded to the call of the Great Commission, "Go ye and preach."

Leaving the comforts of their home and bracing themselves to the challenges of a new and alien land they travelled through whatever means they could get, to reach their final destination-Shangpung, a village in the Jaintia Hills of North East India.

Their three years of mission work had impacted significantly on the lives of the Shangpung community. It was left to their daughter Marilyn to bring out into the open, the work and service of these two dedicated, wonderful souls in the Shangpung village of Jaintia Hills in Meghalaya, based on her parents' diaries and on their letters home to Wales.

The book had its genesis way back in 2003 when I met Marilyn at the RELC Conference, in Singapore. I had presented a paper where I had highlighted the role of the missionaries in contributing to importance of the English Language in the Khasi and Jaintia Hills. Marilyn was among the audience. After the session we met. I remember the glow on Marilyn's face when she said, "My parents were missionaries in Shangpung in the 1930s." That was how our friendship and the bonding began.

The following year we met again in Chiangmai, Bangkok for a Conference organized by the Christian English Language Educators. It was here that the seed of a new venture was conceived when Marilyn introduced two of us from North East India to leaders of an organization that would take an interest in the work of NECTAR in Shillong.

Through that connection and God's mysterious ways, Marilyn became associated with the Teacher Training programme for missionaries organized every year by NECTAR. If Marilyn's parents had shared the gospel with the community, Marilyn was to mentor and prepare teachers not only from Meghalaya but from the north east for mission work in the country and beyond.

It was in one of her visits to Shillong, as part of her work with NECTAR that we both took a trip to Shangpung where she was well received by the congregation of the Shangpung Presbyterian Church. I recall her joy and happiness when she saw the name of her Dad engraved on the Foundation Stone of the Church. It must have been a wonderful experience indeed for Marilyn to be in the very place where her parents had stood many years ago.

As she stood on the Shangpung Church grounds, I believed in my heart that was the time when Marilyn decided to document the wonderful work of her parents in these hills.

Marilyn then set a goal for the completion of the book when we once again met more than once in the following years. The book is indeed a tribute to those who had been so close to her heart. But, the book is also is a rare gift to all of us who had in some way or the other been touched by the lives of the missionaries somewhere, sometime, somehow. It is besides a useful archive for those who are motivated to carry out an in depth study into the contributions of missionaries in our hills.

This book really has three authors: the original writers of the letters and diaries and their daughter.

Marilyn Lewis was born in Wales but has spent most of her adult life in New Zealand as a teacher and teacher educator. She also taught in India and Cambodia during the 1960s and 70s. Now in her retirement from the University of Auckland she enjoys writing (particularly co-writing) books and articles about language learning and teaching. She also runs workshops in various parts of the world.

Dr. T. K. Kharbamon
The EFL University, Shillong Campus

PREFACE

Revival and mission work were a part of my parents' lives from early childhood. My father was carried in a shawl slung over his mother's back to Welsh Revival meetings in Llwynhendy. My mother was "called to the mission field as a girl of eleven at Heath Forward Movement Hall Sunday School, Cardiff" (Fielder, 1983:69), inspired by hearing messages from Dr. Gordon Roberts of Shillong.

After their marriage in June 1933 my parents completed their candidates' training, which included some medical work, and sailed for India in *The City of Venice,* aged 23 and 30. They worked in North East India until early 1939. When they went on furlough that year they left all their possessions behind in Jowai, believing they would be returning. Then, as my mother said in her memoirs, "In September 1939 the unthinkable happened. Our country was at war again." By the war's end they had three children and a parish in Neath, Wales. They never went back to India, and eventually their trunks and crates were returned to them by sea. On India's Independence Day, August 15th 1947, our family set sail for New Zealand.

An exciting event happened towards the end of my mother's long life. At a language teachers' conference in Singapore, I met Dr. T. K. (Lily) Kharbamon from the Shillong Campus of the EFL University. She spoke warmly of the work of the Welsh missionaries and sent my mother a beautiful calendar from the Khasi Hills. That calendar hung on her wall for the last months of her life, giving her a chance to tell visitors about her time in North East India seventy years earlier.

Through Dr. Lily and others, in 2007 an opportunity came for me to visit Shillong, and, even more movingly, the village of Shangpung where my father's name still appears. I put together a brief photographic record to take with me, in the hope that some people might recognise their relatives. This year (1915) in Shillong I was persuaded that a longer account of my parents' time in North East India would be interesting to a number of people.

For most of their years in India my parents wrote weekly letters home to their parents, he in Welsh, she in English, as well as missionary reports to their churches. My mother also typed an almost daily diary. These sources survive as a vast and fading collection of carbon copies on thin paper. Much later my mother's life story, *I remember, I remember* was dictated to me when she was in her late eighties. The two old photograph albums have also helped.

I want to thank Dr. T. K. Kharbamon for pushing this project forward and for being a good friend.

Marilyn Lewis
Auckland, New Zealand

1

THE WELSH MISSION

Before starting on my parents' story it seems a good idea to give a very short background to the work of Welsh missionaries in North East India. When my parents were about to sail in 1933 they were presented with the *History of Christian Missions* (Robinson, 1915) "by a few of their friends and fellow-students as a mark of fellowship and goodwill on their departure to India." The book had been published during World War I and was one of several they collected to prepare them for what they believed would be their life's work. The page and a half on Assam speaks of the work of the Welsh Calvinistic Methodists, started in 1842, in the Khasi and Jaintia Hills, with Shillong as "their principal station" (p. 117). By 1911 the number of converts connected with this mission was said to be 31,000.

A more detailed history of Christian work in that area comes from John Hughes Morris (1930) whose book my parents also read before leaving. According to Morris, in 1842 Thomas Jones and his wife arrived in Cherrapunji, then the government headquarters for the Khasi Hills, after a sea journey of five months. Jones wrote, "The only plan which appears to me likely to answer a good purpose is to establish schools in the various villages to teach the Khasis-children and adults-to read their own language; and to instruct them in the principles of the Christian religion ..." (p. 26). The resulting reading books were described by Morris as "the beginning of Khasi literature" (p. 27). The list of missionary names in the Morris book (Evans, Hughes, Jenkins, Jones, Lewis, Richards, Roberts and Thomas) announced clearly their country of origin.

More background to the Welsh Mission appears in the titles referenced at the end of this book.

2

THE LONG, LONG JOURNEY

The Sea Voyage

Win and Leslie Lewis sailed from Liverpool on *The City of Venice* with other Welsh missionaries, some returning and some first timers. The Adams couple were coming back without their children, who had been left behind with relatives in Milford Haven. My mother told me, years later, that their situation "reinforced my determination not to have children if we were going to have to live without them" (Lewis 1996:115). Dr. Williams and his wife were returning to be in charge of a hospital in Lushai, having left two of their children behind in boarding school. A little girl and a nine month old baby boy travelled with them. With typically Welsh repetition of names, a nurse called Eirlys Williams was heading to India for the first time to be in the same hospital as the Williams couple. David Evans, also a first time missionary, and travelling with his wife Muriel, had been a fellow student of my parents at Cardiff University.

On Board the City of Venice

The Land Journey

The last part of the journey to North East India was a mixture of river and rail transport. After reaching Calcutta they left the ship and boarded a boat up the river. My mother's meticulously typed daily diary allows us to follow their progress day by day, and in some cases hour by hour.

About 1 o'clock we were awakened by the stopping of the engines at the mouth of the Hoogly River, to take on the pilot. The Hoogly River has shifting sandbanks, which make it very difficult to navigate.

Sunday, 19th November

In Calcutta they stayed in the Lee Memorial hostel, an American Mission House described as having a strongly Christian atmosphere. The couple running the hostel had lost all but one of their children in an earthquake that destroyed their hill station school. The one child who initially survived died of tetanus not long afterwards. Now the hostel was named in the children's memory.

Part of their time in Calcutta was spent collecting supplies, including a bicycle each, which they had been told would be necessary for their work. There is no mention in later diaries of these bicycles being ridden and in fact every description of the paths and roads suggests that bicycles would have been of little use. Horses seemed to be the answer. They met Katie Hughes, a missionary who had trained a Lushai choir of girls and boys to sing the *Messiah*. They were now on a tour of Northern India, having left their own area for the first time. Their concert was broadcast.

On Wednesday 22nd November, after an early breakfast, taxis arrived at 6:45 a.m. for them and their nine packages. With two packages per coolie they must have made an impressive sight. The previous day had been my father's 30th birthday, but my mother writes regretfully that it escaped her memory.

The train took their party along the Assam-Bengal railway first across tree covered plains until at one o'clock they joined a river steamer which stopped at many places up the Ganges. Their deck class accommodation gave beautiful views along a "very wide and glassy" river, so wide in fact that it looked to them like a lake. After dinner they left the boat at 8 p.m. for an overnight rail journey. As a happy coincidence, the ticket inspector on the train was a Christian, originally from Maulvi Bazaar, who knew many of the missionaries. At Assam they changed trains.

Their party became smaller each time people reached their destinations, or at least the nearest railway station. First the Adams couple left and then David and Muriel Edwards who were headed for Shaistaganj where Miss Laura Evans met them. Next it was my parents' turn to leave the train. At Srimongol, the nearest station to Maulvi, they were met by Mr. and Mrs. Roberts, the senior missionaries, with another change of transport. The Roberts' car jolted them along the fourteen mile road to Maulvi which was described as less of a road than a dusty cart-track. The Roberts couple were to feature frequently and with admiration in their accounts of work for the next few years.

Welcome to Maulvi Bazaar

Maulvi Bazaar was on the plains in South Sylhet, 35 miles to the south of Sylhet town and a few miles north of the Assam-Bengal Railway. It was remembered by my mother as being "on the plains where rice was the crop, with tea gardens in the one or two undulating areas" (Lewis, 1996:123).

With a population of 3,334 in 1930 Maulvi Bazaar, now in Bangladesh, was the smallest town in Sylhet. Morris (1930) tells us that the mission station had opened there in 1907 but when he was writing there had been no resident missionary since the death of Mr. Pengwern Jones in 1927. Jones had sailed for India in November 1887 with his first wife, who died from cholera within a week of arriving in Sylhet. He remarried and continued to work in that area for forty years.

Two years after his death a Memorial Chapel, which my parents would come to know, was opened in his memory. It also commemorated an evangelist by the name of Jacob Emded, previously a Mohammedan, who had been baptised and then put through a course of training. The money for the chapel had been contributed by friends in India and in Wales, as explained in these words over the entrance. "Built in answer to prayer and opened free from debt." Rev. Jones had planned the chapel for gospel and other meetings.

The November, 1933 welcome to this new young missionary couple, the first since his death, was warm and memorable.

An arch had been made at the entrance of greenery with paper decorations and the text "Blessed is he that cometh in the name of the Lord." As we drove in some crackers were let off. When we alighted from the car onto the verandah of the bungalow we were greeted by the pastor and by one of the evangelists who knows English..... It was obviously a welcome from their hearts and I was very moved (24th November, 1933).

The welcome continued more formally,

All the Christians had gathered together and one or two who were not Christians. There were perhaps 40 in all... The church is over a mile away, so the Christians usually meet in a bamboo hut on the compound....

The pastor was chairman, and several of the men made welcome speeches. Mr. Roberts was interpreter. The chief points in all the speeches were these: their great love and high esteem for Mr. and Mrs. Pengwern Jones, how much they had missed them and how they had been praying for a successor to them, how overjoyed they were when they heard that we were coming and how they had prayed much for us that we should be given health to stay among us.

However, settling in had to wait. After a quick look at Maulvi Bazaar, they went on to Sylhet for their orientation under the guidance of the Roberts couple.

3

ORIENTATION IN SYLHET

In the 1930s Sylhet town was part of the wider area of North East India also known as Sylhet. The town was 50 miles north of Maulvi Bazaar, but mentioning the distance doesn't do justice to the 1933 journey which included crossing three bridgeless rivers. The procedure was for the car to be driven down a steep bank onto a ferry boat and up the other side again. When there were bridges, these were made of bamboo. On the way they called at a Bible School for evangelists at Patera and also at an outstation where two evangelists had their headquarters.

My mother spoke glowingly of Sylhet, where they stayed in a bungalow "on the top of a little hill, with a line of beautifully wooded hills opposite and the high Khasi Hills in the distance." In Wales, the town's name was associated with the Rev. Pengwern Jones, but by the 1930s the mission hostesses were M. P. Jones and Hetty Evans. The newcomers' time was spent finding out about the language, customs and mission work they were to be part of.

The Roberts Couple

Mr. Roberts was a long-serving missionary in Sylhet who had been in India for thirty years. He was "getting on for sixty," which no doubt seemed elderly to someone in her twenties.

Mr. Roberts' strength was in organising all sorts or projects to finance the work. For instance he set up a bus company using Christian drivers.

The couple's hospitality and kindness were frequently mentioned with gratitude, as in this extract from February, 1936 when my parents were again passing through Sylhet.

Mr. and Mrs. Roberts are real marvels in the way of arranging for people. I have never seen anyone more unselfish than they, and willing to put themselves out, especially when any rush and crowd takes its toll of Mrs. Roberts-but she does not show that to people.

Amongst Mr. Roberts' many duties was preaching. During a visit to Shillong in September 1936 there was a chance to hear him preach twice, in Bengali at the morning service and in an English language service at night.

He preached on "They that wait upon the Lord," and illustrated the meaning of waiting in this context by the king's lords-in-waiting whose job it is not to sit down and do nothing but to wait upon the king to find out his every wish and make them known to the world and see that they are executed.

In the evening his text was "If any man be in Christ he is a new creature." He opened by a reference to the Hindu doctrine of retribution: what you sow you reap. He pointed out that that was the law of nature, but that the central truth of Christianity was that God in Christ sowed such a crop of good by his life and death that we are able to reap from this and by such reaping the fruit of our own sowing can be turned from calamity to discipline.

Later Mr. Roberts would supervise the work at Maulvi Bazaar after my parents left for Shangpung.

Sylhet Routines

On the first Sunday, 26th November 1933, they joined in the regular Sylhet routines, which included Sunday School in the morning in the Lines, as the district with the police quarters was called. Hetty Evans ran this Sunday School. There was also a service at night. My parents were amongst the youngest missionaries, some of the others being well past the age of retirement. Speaking of a very uncomfortable house they visited, my mother writes that.

Miss Evans [Hetty] has lived there all these years and never said a word about it [the heat and the closeness of the railway line]. Her powers of endurance are really remarkable; she does some things that one would consider beyond human endurance, and yet she has lived to be over seventy-a truly remarkable thing on these plains.

Hetty Evans had a small group of girls training at an industrial school to be self-supporting later in their villages. They lived in the compound and started their day with prayers before lessons in "the three Rs." Apart from breaks they worked until four on various tasks of bread making, weaving, fancywork, dressmaking, knitting and mending. Looms and sewing machines were provided. Some of their work was for the boys in the industrial school and some was sold. The end of the day didn't mark the end of their work though. Each girl had her own garden plot to work on in the evenings.

Some Lushai Christians lived there with their families. Miss Evans led a Bible Class with them every Sunday morning using as an interpreter the one man who knew a little English. Three weeks later my mother had a chance to take the class when Hetty Evans was away. It was fascinating to me to read that "some men from the Assam Rifles" turned up, because more than seventy years later the Training Centre in Shillong where I did some teacher training (NECTAR) was quite near to their headquarters. To my mother they seemed "great strapping men."

In early December "they went with Mr. Roberts to a little church belonging to the mission on the other side of the town." Although, it had been the start of the Mission there, the congregation was now down to only two families. My mother was able to say a few words to them because they could understand English.

At a tea garden church a mid-week service was planned to welcome them.

Picture us driving along a country lane in the dark, then trying to back the car in a side-track by the aid of a flash-lamp. ... walking carefully over a bridge made of three bamboo poles, walking along a little path, passing a circle of rice that had been threshed during the day by oxen, then reaching the little church.

The grass-roofed building had bamboo walls, covered to halfway up with soft concrete, the upper half loosely woven with bamboo. Lighting was from an oil lamp. The congregation were coolies whose "pitiful" wages were 6 to 7 rupees a month. As an extra they gathered wood to sell in the bazaar. Everyone was wrapped in a warm garment. Despite their sad economic state these people were described as the most alive church in the whole district.

The members are most enthusiastic. Many of them have tiny little plots of land round their houses and the first-fruits of everything they grow is brought to the church to be dedicated to the Lord. Last year, owing to the depression, the collections were down a little. As soon as this was known a few of the members made up the sum out of their poverty.

In mid-December my father toured the Maulvi district under Mr. Roberts' guidance. While he was away Mrs. Roberts took my mother round the compound to meet people in the various houses. She also visited the girls' school run by Phyllis Jones, who is described as "very efficient" despite meagre resources. Pupils were graded by achievement rather than by age, since they started at different times.

On his return, my father had a good report of his tour.

Les has been round the villages in our district and says it is going to be lovely working there. There is plenty to do and the head evangelist [Nabo] is a very good worker. He also met a number of the tea planters as he went round.

Gratitude for Nabo featured frequently in their letters home.

Other Workers

Various photographs record their time in Sylhet, including one of Phyllis Morgan, Hetty Evans and my mother.

Another, also taken in Sylhet in late 1933 shows my mother, Muriel Evans and Phyllis Morgan at the back and in front David Edwards, Hetty Evans, Mr. Roberts and my father.

The following photograph that also appears on this book's cover includes Back row Mrs. Roberts, Mrs. Bannerjee, Mrs. Dutta, my mother Front row Mr. Ghose, Mr. Dutta (Sylhet late1933)

Christmas, 1933

Christmas Day was long and busy, starting at 4 a.m. when they were woken by the sound of singing, as people walked round and round the compound. For the 9 o'clock English language service quite a few Europeans turned up. Then it was back to the compound for their own service.

The school bus had been sent out to get the Christians from the outlying churches and numbers were swelled still more by a contingent of Lushai soldiers from the Assam Rifles. The children sat on the floor in front and benches had to be put on the verandah outside to accommodate the overflow. By the end of the service there were crowds of passers-by who had been attracted....

The service was opened by the young men's reading and praying-three for each. Then there was a long Bengali sermon by a country pastor... Then there was a story for the children by our pundit's wife. [who taught in the high school]. ... The next item was a hymn sung by the Lushais. It was ever so nice to hear all the soldiers singing. A Lushai student from the hostel on the compound gave them an address in Lushai. The poor men deserved something good after listening for so long to a foreign tongue. .

That evening they went to a different kind of service where

...... a small tea garden church had invited the missionaries and young people of Sylhet to join them in their special Christmas service. A five-mile drive brought us to the tea garden, then we had a short walk to reach the church. It was a bright moonlit night and as we approached we could see the outlines of three buildings. These were the church and the houses of the two Christian families who are the sole members of the church. ....

The strains of... singing now fell upon our ears and when we had passed through the arches of banana branches... we came across the young people seated in a circle on the ground, chanting hymns to Bengali tunes. One of their number sang a line, then the others responded in chorus. The only illumination they had, besides the moonlight, was a hurricane lantern. It was a most striking picture and I wished I could have had a snap of it.

When the singing was over we entered the church, a bamboo hut no larger than the room of an ordinary house. Two bamboo poles were the pillars.... The congregation sat on the floor. The Sylhet portion of it was not over rich but they were gorgeously apparelled compared with the local people, who were practically in rags although it was a cold night.... The meeting consisted in hymn singing, open prayer, Scripture recitations, a story for the children, and an address.

We can assume that all attenders were included in the feast that followed.

At the end of the meeting came the feast, out on the ground in the moonlight. The main part of the meal was rice and curry, to be eaten with the fingers. The cooking was done in big brass bowls on the ground, over a fire. The guests sat in two rows and ate off banana leaves. I thought it was one the most thrilling sights I had ever seen and I felt reluctant to leave.

Since Christmas Eve that year was a Sunday, the children had been given their Christmas cards and calendars the day before. These were received with excitement despite being in English. My mother had one thought about these gifts.

I hear now that it is possible to get such things printed in Bengali from a publishing house in London. That would really be a much better idea.

Fortunately her suggestion was never followed, because later she noted how exciting it was for children to open packages that had been lovingly wrapped by well-wishers in Wales.

Festivities continued on Boxing Day with a wedding. The groom was an evangelist lately out from college and the bride was the sister of one of the teachers at the Girls' School, not more than 17 years old. Apparently the matter of girls' marriage age was controversial, the school's policy being that they should be sixteen before marrying. Grooms, on the other hand, were over thirty.

December 1933 Wedding

Eventually my parents set off for their first home, although they would pass through Sylhet from time to time en route to other places.

4

MAULVI BAZAAR
THEIR FIRST STATION

The First Home

My parents lived in a bungalow on the compound, which was their first home had since their wedding less than a year earlier.

A team of people helped them in their daily lives, with some responsibilities going beyond the domestic. Shanwah they said is mentioned as learning a verse every week to recite in Sunday School.

Leslie Lewis with Colleagues in Maulvi Bazaar, March 1934

An alarm in mid-January came at a time when my mother was in bed with a fever.

I was just enjoying the bit of quiet when the bed began to shake. I thought the foundations of the house had been disturbed by all the banging. [Alterations were being made to the bungalow].

Naba and Les appeared at the window to tell me to get out of the house quickly. There was an earthquake and it wasn't safe to stay indoors.

The effects in their town were minor, but when the newspapers arrived they told a different story for other districts where lives were lost and houses destroyed.

Visitors passing through Maulvi Bazaar, announced or unannounced, were a feature of life there. A week after the earthquake Mr. Goshe, principal of the Evangelists' Theological College at Patera called unexpectedly during a vacation tour with three of his students.

Medical Work

Regular medical work included attending to patients who came from the village to Naba in the dispensary. Naba was the evangelist-dispenser, "a mature and energetic Christian" although only thirty years old, who had been trained at the Sylchar hospital.

Rather than his depending upon us, we have depended upon him. He is ready to spend himself for his Lord and forgoes many of the pleasures of this life in order to serve him the more wholeheartedly.

Naba, Dispenser and Evangelist

[Naba's training] *made him quite experienced in treating the sick, although he wasn't a doctor. He became a special friend. Because he had the idea that we should make some use of the compound, he and Les put their heads together and came up with the idea of growing pineapples.*

Patients came daily, often from long distances, preferring to visit them than to go to official doctors. A small price was charged for medicines, but tracts and Gospels were given out free to those who were interested.

Leprosy Patient and his Wife
March 1934

A Khasi midwife lived just outside their compound, but her district was so large that she could attend only urgent cases. Occasionally, my mother found herself involved in delivering babies when she accompanied the midwife on her rounds.

One birth took place on the floor of a room totally smoke-filled from a fire. It must have been the end of the cold weather. In the middle of the birth the midwife was summoned to attend the wife of some more important village person. She pointed out to me that although the other woman was far from the last stages of labour she would have to go. I sent quickly for the dispenser so he could stand outside and shout instructions in to me. Meanwhile they called in a village midwife with the filthiest clothes imaginable. So, much for all the sterile instruments the other midwife had left. This substitute person whipped out a rusty penknife and cut the cord. The mother fainted soon afterwards, but they did manage to get her through to the bedroom.

(Lewis 1996:121-2)

Another time the midwife took me along to a Muslim house where she was to deliver a baby. She was taken everywhere in the taxi her husband ran. We found the whole extended family gathered. I was taken aside and fed before being taken into the women's quarters. The man's first wife had died in childbirth only a year earlier but he'd quickly found this 15-year-old second wife. She took no notice at all of her husband when he passed through but when her father, who was an important man in his village, arrived she told him she was about to die. That didn't happen. What did go wrong for her was that the baby was a girl. She turned her face to the wall to try and ignore it. They didn't all react like that. I saw one new mother put her baby daughter straight to the breast.

In January 1935, the cook announced that "his wife was expecting a baby that day and would I please go with Philte (the midwife)." Off they went on the two mile walk.

On the way a messenger met us to say that the cook's father, a very old man, had fallen down unconscious and was now unable to speak or walk. The poor cook was terribly upset. By the time we reached the old man he was able to speak just a little. Phillte thought the doctor should be sent for, so I wrote him a note, and in a couple of hours the cook returned with him. He said that the old man's blood pressure was very high and his heart weak .....

When the old man's condition was no better next day, the cook was given time off to go home and have time with him.

On that or a later occasion the 12 year old wife of the cook gave birth to a baby with a club foot. It was decided that when she was a year old she could be taken to the Mission Hospital. The father agreed, but not all of the village women thought it was a good idea, so it didn't happen.

1934 Assembly

Because forward planning was part of the work of the Welsh Presbyterian Mission, from time to time regular duties were put on hold for meetings such as the annual assemblies. In early 1934 it was the turn of Maulvi Bazaar to host the Plains Assembly in the town a mile or more away in the Pengwern Jones memorial church building mentioned earlier. Thirteen missionaries and 150-200 Indians attended. Some of the missionaries were accommodated in my parents' bungalow, including the 78 year old Mr. Evans who, despite some deafness and short-sightedness, was willing to join in activities including a game of badminton.

Even for newcomers like my parents whose Bengali language let them down "the Spirit was so manifest that we could feel His presence and were greatly blessed." There was a reason for this feeling.

The Indian delegates were up at 6 a.m. or earlier, holding group prayer meetings, and the Holy Spirit was manifestly present throughout the whole Assembly. We had not expected much blessing for ourselves as we would not be able to understand the language of the meeting. Yet, though the proceedings were unintelligible to us, we felt unmistakably the presence of the Holy Spirit, and were blessed thereby. How wonderful that God is not bound by human limitations.... (6th April, 1934).

The speaker on this occasion was Dr. Helen Rowlands, "a leading Bengali scholar much admired by Indians for her extraordinary proficiency in this language." Perhaps not surprisingly, given her my mother's lack of Bengali, she reports in detail only on the sermons given in English. These were by Rev. W. Morgan of Silchar, Rev. E. Adams of Karimganj and Rev. J. W. Roberts of Sylhet.

Language Studies

Private lessons

As part of their daily work my parents took Bengali lessons with a local Hindu, who said "he had put a photo of Jesus up alongside his Hindu gods at home" (p. 123). Perhaps he was influenced by the textbook, which was *The life of Christ* in Bengali. Despite these lessons, impatience at their lack of progress shows through in letters home.

We are still unable to do any missionary work, owing to our ignorance of Bengali. It will be at least a year before we are able to preach, but we speak occasionally to the Christians through an interpreter (March 1934).

Language school in Darjeeling

That first year they went to language school in Darjeeling to learn Bengali. The course ran from April to June with one day off to celebrate the King's birthday on 4th June Darjeeling was the hill station for the whole of Bengal and particularly for the Governor in the hot season. The journey started by car, then continued by train.

There are no trains in the hills, except for [the] hill section which goes via Haflong to Upper Assam. It is rather an interesting railway. It was built for strategic purposes, as we are on the border of India. The fact that it goes uphill, the number of bridges and tunnels, the frequent landslides, necessitating that a trolley always runs ahead of the train in case of danger, all prevent the railway from being a paying proposition, and now they say that it couldn't even be much good for strategic purposes, as an enemy could easily take possession of the tunnels etc.

It is interesting to note that reference was made to an enemy rather than the enemy. Defence purposes are mentioned again in a note from late 1936.

In these border districts a change is made from broad to narrow gauge, the idea being that an enemy could not use the railway because the carriages that fit in one place wouldn't fit lower down. But now they say that it is a mixed blessing because the defenders would be in a similar difficulty.

The journey continued by steamer, and the Calcutta mail train as far as Siliguri. Finally they went by taxi up, up and up to the cool air of the hills.

The period at Language School was a rich time for them for two reasons, one, of course, being the chance to improve their basic Bengali. Progress was measured by fortnightly tests, with the final assessment coming in November when everyone would go to Calcutta for the examination. The other source of richness was the fellowship of their fellow students. Life in Darjeeling was not all about study. My mother was one of those who enjoyed horse riding in their times off, and of course there was always shopping. There is mention of Chinese people coming with goods every Saturday. It would be interesting to know their history and whether they lived there or travelled to and fro.

At the end of the course in June a taxi took them down again to Siliguri for the start of their return journey by rail. They left at 5 p.m. for an overnight journey. Next day they woke up in good time (2 a.m.!) in order to change trains at Paradah. By 5 a.m. they were at the river, ready for the steamer. This was the rainy season.

The countryside is largely under flood now, and it is amazing to see how many of the houses are marooned. (Thurs 28th June).

In the pattern of the mixed transport they had become accustomed to, by 9 p.m. they had left the steamer and were once more on a train.

Examination in Calcutta

With the November examination looming in Calcutta, preparation became important. In October, her friend Helen and Mr. Ghose gave them a mock oral test of three parts: story telling based on pictures, reading aloud and then a conversation. It sounds remarkably like an oral language test today.

Finally, on Friday 6th November, it was time to leave for Calcutta.

We went down this time by a different route, going down the other side of the Khasi Hills, crossing the Brahmaputra by steamer, then going westwards by train along the upper valley, joining the Darjeeling Line and so down to Calcutta. Although, as the crow flies this is a longer distance, it is actually an easier journey.

In Calcutta they met their fellow students and their Darjeeling teacher, Mr. Frazer, his German wife and their three young children. He was a lecturer at the Baptist University College.

Their time was divided between shopping and last minute study until the examination day arrived. There was one brief interruption during the drive to the location.

When we were nearing Cossipore our car, along with others nearby, was stopped and we were sent to the side of the road. We wondered at first what was the matter, but we were not long left in doubt. In the distance we saw two huge headlights of a car, and we guessed that it was either the Viceroy, who was in Calcutta at the time, or the governor.

Their guess was right. The Viceroy and Lady Willingdon sped past preceded by a motor cycle and side car with armed police and then followed by an open car full of armed detectives plus more motorbikes. Meanwhile the road was lined by mounted and unmounted police. As my mother noted, "you can imagine how that sort of thing annoys ardent nationalists."

The Church in Maulvi Bazaar

Back in Maulvi Bazaar, my parents started using the local language during worship with their church congregation of five families. A small building on the compound was their meeting place.

All the people involved in the Christian work lived in the compound and that's where we had services for them, along with one or two other people like the midwife. The floor of the little worship building was dried cow dung and the walls were woven bamboo. The missionary would do the introduction and the Indian pastor would preach. In the front seat there would be all the children, then men on one side and women on the other. That was their tradition, not the missionaries' idea.

After a couple of years, my father's Bengali must have been considered strong enough for him to play a bigger part in the service. Perhaps an interpreter was available.

Les preached today and made it a children's service, getting a boy and girl to read the scriptures. Much more seems to be expected of children in this country, at least in the Christian community, than of children of the same ages at home. Little Philip, Maya Babu's boy, is only seven, but takes part in the verse-by-verse reading with the adults in prayers every morning, and leads in prayer like an adult... I must say that the children are very well behaved in service. They will sit through a long sermon, with its translation, without moving or speaking the whole of the time and that although they sit in a row by themselves" [Sunday 8th March, 1936].

From time to time my mother reflected, as she had with the children's Christmas presents in Sylhet, on the value of sending parcels from Wales. These were packed and posted faithfully from supporters, including a Miss Jane Jones of Pwlleli who sent a package full of calendars, texts, verses and even a Sunday school register with a page of "very helpful hints to teachers." Some of the materials sound as if they would be useful today: transfer books, paint books, crayons, Christmas cards and story books. It wasn't the fault of the kind Miss Jones that everything was in English.

These mission parcels from home are a great problem. The carriage and duty on them is often more than their worth, especially now when so many things can be bought in India. And yet preparing the parcels often provides work for missionary circles.

However, on reflection she thought that asking for money instead would create less interest in the work by Welsh church members.

Shillong Holiday

In September, 1934 at the end of the hot weather my parents took their first holiday in Shillong in a bungalow built for the purpose. Reaching there took some time, travelling by car, bus, river boat, train, some of them more than once. Her family at home were not spared any details of the journey. The first day started with an hour by car and then the train until 4.30.

Next day it was the train again from 10 a.m. to 6 p.m. until they set off up the hill by car. This final road journey was "steep and winding with many blind corners." Their description has come to my mind during my times of making the same climb up from Guwahati, but in a comfortable taxi along the developing four lane highway. Most recently, in February 2015, my visit coincided with *The Shillong*

Times printing a number of articles and letters complaining about the time it took to reach the capital of Meghalaya from the plains, whereas the other state capitals had seven day a week, all weather airports. My parents would have found the four lane highway the height of luxury.

Shanwah, who worked in and around the house for them, was on the journey too, being described as "becoming quite like a son of ours." We have to hope that he had time to enjoy Shillong in between being left in charge of my father who had a recurrence of malaria. The time in Shillong gave insights into some of the other missionaries' work, as we see in the next chapter.

Schools

Back in Maulvi Bazaar, once they had learned enough language, my parents had a number of roles, including establishing schools in the tea plantations for the children of the coolies. Also, by February, 1935 they had started a little village school on the compound, with Maya Babu's wife as the teacher and over forty children.

A group of children and their teacher captured by the camera in November, 1935 seem to have their eyes on something important. Could it be that a classmate was running late for the photograph? Perhaps some people today will recognise the faces of their grandparents in this photograph.

As well as their own students my parents had contact with high school boys from the town who enjoyed the chance to improve their English. That included attending the church services on the compound from time to time.

Visits around Maulvi Bazaar

By October of their first year they were over the really hot weather for a few months and the pattern of their regular lives returned after the breaks at Language School and Shillong. This pattern included paying home visits.

There were often surprises about how much or how little people had travelled. On the one hand, the paniwallah had been to England as a fireman on a steamer and yet the chowkidar, who took them to visit their unwell cook in his village, about a quarter of a mile from the chowkidar's, had not been to that district since childhood.

For my mother the worst part of the two mile walk to the cook's village was the bridge made of single bamboos with large gaps between them. Added to that problem the bamboo was very slippery and there was nothing to hang onto. However, once they reached the cook's house things looked up.

We suddenly found ourselves in a delightful little courtyard with neat little houses on each side..... The floor is kept clean and fresh with frequent plasterings with cowdung (which by the way is the material of which our church floor is made).

They were welcomed by the cook and his pregnant 14 year old wife. It seemed that when the cook was thinking of becoming a Christian the family quickly found him a wife so as to keep him close to them.

Another time the visit was to the chokidar's village to see his month old baby, a walk of only about 15 minutes. Again, a bamboo bridge was a challenge.

For visits further afield there was river transport.

Travelling round the district by boat

Duties ranged from sorting out quarrels, to burying the dead plus some once-off events. For example, there was the husband whose patience ran out with his wife's frequent infidelities and who tried to use a dagger to settle the matter. When it reached the point that he had taken all the house furniture to sell, someone sent for the missionary. In this case it seems a reconciliation was arranged.

Then there was the role of hosting visitors. Dr. and Mrs. John Williams of the Lushai Hospital arrived in the middle of the domestic uproar just mentioned down the road but "they took it very nicely." The Williams couple were visiting the stations on their way back from a special course in Calcutta. The word 'course' might refer to medical treatment. Mrs. Williams talked of how the Lushai church members had met for long and regular prayer meetings during her husband's serious illness a year earlier. In February, 1935 there was a weekend visit from the Sidney Evans couple during their tour of the plains. This was a chance to hear first-hand news from Cherrapunji and especially of the Theological College where he was principal.

Some calls on the missionaries' services were demanding in a different way.

At two o'clock a letter came from the SDO to say that a European had died the night before in Srimongol. A planter had been informed but had not replied so now they wanted Les to see to the burial.

The deceased was an Anglo Indian and he had died of malaria while staying in the dak bungalow. There was not a penny found on him, so who knows what he must have suffered.

This time a delay to the journey was caused by the weather, rather than by elephants which are mentioned elsewhere. The rain was beating into the car, which had no side screens, so they sheltered under some trees, trying not to think about lightning and falling branches. At the police station in Srimongol they were told the planter had replied saying he would attend to the burial, although he still hadn't arrived.

A one-off duty occurred in January, 1936 when one of the Christians came in with a rumour that King George V. was dead. Anyone born in the late 20th century will find it difficult to believe how long it took to verify this news. True, the radio (wireless) had been invented, but as they noted on a later visit to Shillong, keeping it in a fit state was a work of patience. It had been some time before they knew that in October, 1935 Mussolini was invading Abyssinia. My mother often spoke of reading the most recent papers first and trying to make sense of what had happened earlier. Looking ahead, when the next king, Edward VIII, abdicated later that year no whisper of the scandal reached them until it had all happened. It wasn't just the distance that held up the news. The British newspapers had kept very quiet about the details of the royal doings until the last minute.

Confirmation of the king's death came next day when they saw the flag outside the court flying at half-mast. Sure enough, he had died at Sandringham. A few days later the Europeans asked the missionary to take a memorial service. I couldn't help smiling at the picture of my father, who had Welsh Nationalist leanings before that party existed, preparing a sermon to honour an English monarch. The service attracted the crowds.

When we went along to the church we were simply amazed, as was everyone else, to see the great number present. There were 45 in the corps, and the others present made it up to between eighty and a hundred, a thing never known before in living memory. The cars were such as I had never seen in India. I had no idea that there were so many Europeans living in the district….. Although, it was so difficult to preach a sermon under those circumstances (and it was a sermon he was asked for, not a mere address) he really managed to speak appropriately to the occasion and to convey a spiritual message at the same time.

Following the service they were invited along to the Club.

Namashudra Villages

Once they had a visit from ten young men representing a group of Namashudra (depressed class) villages who wanted to hold a series of joint meetings where the missionaries would instruct them on how to better their conditions. Some also wanted to become Christians although they feared, unless there was a mass movement, that they would suffer from the other villagers. [For more details on these villages, see the notes in Chapter 5 from the handwritten pages].

Four people set out for the journey to those villages: Naba Babu, Mr. Ghose and the two Lewises. It was supposed to be ten miles in a seven seater, 24 horse power car driven by my father, and then three miles on foot, although the three miles turned out to be eight. They dared not drink any of their water supply despite their desperate thirst, in case of an accident, when the water would be even more necessary.

So on we trudged, getting more and more exhausted; in places our way led over ploughed fields and that made walking very difficult.

By the end of the walk their skin was burned, their tongues swollen and their eyes bloodshot. Finally there was a three hour meeting. My father had thrown aside thoughts of safe water and drank from a stagnant pool where people bathed. Not surprisingly he became ill on the way back and had to be carried on a stretcher to a ferry to finish the journey.

The Tea Plantations

As we see several times in the diaries, the tea plantations were a source of contacts between missionaries, other Europeans and Indians. On one occasion (April 1935) the manager of a plantation sixteen miles away initiated a visit from the missionaries to his Christian workers. The distance didn't seem too far but there was a hitch when one of two elephants on the road in front of them took fright at the car and bolted across the rice fields. The manager was described as a bachelor, the son of a clergyman "and very good to the coolies."

It seemed that the European wives of some of the tea planters had rather lonely lives, with "nothing to do but frequent the Club in the evenings." There was one interesting insight into the double standards of some people working for the tea companies. A British man married an Indian woman after living with her for some time. Once they were married, the tea company dismissed him, having had no trouble with the earlier arrangement, which left the man trying to make a living out of a plantation he set up for himself.

News of a tea garden with a difference came when they met the Aie family on a visit to Shillong. He was a Danish planter with a wife and five-year-old daughter.

Some time in the last century their mission obtained land in Upper Assam in which to settle the Santhals, a hill tribe in Bihar, amongst whom they were working, because the land in which they were living was too poor to support them. After a time a tea planter in the district, who was sympathetic with their work, suggested that they open up a tea garden and offered to look after it. This was quite a success until his death.

Then difficulties began because the planters whom the mission engaged were not religious men-they gave the coolies beer etc etc. So, in the end they had to have missionaries from Denmark to take on the work. Mr. Aie is both a planter and a missionary.

It is interesting to read of this arrangement, sometimes referred to these days as tent-making, because today North East Indian Christians travel to other countries in similar dual roles.

Tea plantation workers from Madras who had churches of their own.

The teacher who was incharge of the largest of these churches and who was an old man, died a little while ago. Now the church is without pastoral oversight; the people are mostly Madrassis ...and it is desirable that they have a Madrassi leader, as the late teacher was.

The replacement teacher, who had been training for 18 months while working in a village, went to the plantation with his wife and three little children. He seems to have made a good impression on the local workers during a preliminary visit to organise his new home. A woman attending a prayer meeting for him remarked that, despite his educated status, he had "set to himself with a spade and other implements, just like a coolie" to prepare the premises for his family.

The Silchar Assembly 1936

In 1936, it was the turn of Silchar to host the Assembly. Instead of the usual train journey "we had decided on the adventurous plan of driving all the way." This involved a drive of 100 miles, which would be a day's journey. The party of four included Naba Babu and Maya Babu plus their luggage of suitcases, a hat box, bedding, blankets, a camp bed and mattresses. Fitting these and the passengers into the vehicle was only the start of their concerns.

The condition of the roads was the next challenge.

There are three types of roads. Those that run through open fields are built up high like banks to prevent them from flooding. The animals grazing in the fields are constantly crossing from one side to the other.... The second type of road is that running between houses. These [the houses] are concealed by trees so that one can rarely see them, and children have a dangerous habit of suddenly popping out .... That means slow driving all the time and frequent pulling up. The third kind of road is that running through tea gardens and jungle. Here it is twists and rises and dips that cause the bother....

The next delay was not predicted. It's hard not to smile at travellers who remembered a hat box but forget a driving licence.

We had only gone a short distance when Les thought of his licence. He does not carry it about with him as a rule, but it was a bit risky to go to a big place like Silchar without it so we had to go back for it. Then there was the usual delay while we crossed the river, and at last we were on the road again.

A further hold-up happened when they came across a bus accident.

We had only been going for about ten minutes when we noticed a great crowd in front, and a man came rushing up in a state of great excitement saying there was an accident, and then we noticed, in a ditch, a bus smashed to bits. Les and Naba Babu immediately threw off their coats and rushed along. There were nine people in the bus, each of whom was seen in turn.

People taken from the wreckage had to be triaged into the very seriously injured, those with fractures, and a third group with bad cuts (which meant the danger of tetanus). Once some wounds had been attended to, and those who wanted it were given tea from the flasks my parents were carrying, the injured were loaded into two other buses that had arrived, ready to be transported back to the dispensary at Maulvi Bazaar. Apparently, it was no use offering seats in the car because there would have been no room for the injured to lie down.

The cause of the accident (a woman running out in front of the bus) was not far from my mother's mind as they started up again, but the next hold-up was of a different type again. During a roadside tea break they had removed the screw from the water cylinder to top it up. Some time further on it was found to be missing.

The only thing to do was to go back and look for it, but alas, in trying to turn in a very narrow place, the self-starter got jammed; and then when we got out to push the car, there was the missing screw on the foot-board. However, the damage was done. The car would yield to neither self-starter, handle or pushing. We were indeed in a hole, being miles from a railway station, none of us knowing anything about the workings of the car, and no one to help us.

The solution was to send a small boy with a note to the nearest planter, two miles away to ask "if he had a mechanic in his factory who would help us." Not knowing whether "the promise of a big reward" would work with the young messenger, my father decided to have one more go himself. Although, my father was handy with woodwork (in fact some of his works still survive) and had spent a very short time working down a Welsh coal mine, motor vehicles were new to him. Unfortunately his efforts made the situation worse and the party took refuge from the sun by sitting on the floor-board while they waited. The European planters were not strangers to them. Missionaries had to ask their permission to set up schools for the children of the coolies.

About two hours later help arrived.

We heard the hum of a car and the planter appeared. It did not take him two minutes to discover the root of the trouble and unscrew the offending part. Then he drove us back with it to his bungalow and showed Les how to put it right again. Then he gave us a wash and, to our great surprise, lunch, which I must say was very refreshing.

In the end, with darkness looming, the car had to be left at the railway station and the journey finished in the same way as it had started for all the other Assembly delegates-by train.

Once they finally arrived at the Assembly, a number of activities are mentioned. My mother had to report on the previous year's Rice Collection. "It was a bit of a trial expressing the figures in Bengali, because Bengali numbers are the hardest I have known in any language." (She had some experience of counting in English, Welsh, Latin, Greek, Hebrew, Hindi and Khasi as well as Bengali).

Messages delivered in English, such as one by Rev. William Davies, were interpreted into Bengali by one of the missionaries, Helen Rowlands, whose language skills have already been noted as excellent.

The 1936 Commission from Wales

1936 opened with a New Year's Day service to welcome The Commission, a group from Wales who came to review the work of the Mission in North East India. Their visit was to have a major impact on the work. Although it was the cold season, when people might be expected to tolerate longer services, the welcome formalities were kept short since "they have probably had their fill of welcome speeches."

The Maulvi Bazaar part of the visit ended without any definite announcements of changes. These would come later. However, hints were dropped that the work was not flourishing. Each member of the Commission gave a short speech, and when it was the turn of Principal Phillips he "emphasised that however discouraging the work might be the thing to do was to follow God's guidance with confidence, but never to try to move things along faster by following our own ideas, as that would be sure to bring disappointment in the long run." (Jan 1st 1936). Part of the situation was that a large number of buildings had accumulated in various parts of the plain, not all of them currently being used for Mission work.

However, the Commission members shared their thoughts with the missionaries informally "much more openly… than I should have expected… Their conversation seems to indicate that they are going to advocate the closing down of a good deal of the work on the Plains, leaving it in the hands of Indian workers, and one or two of the centres only in the hands of missionaries."

My father drove the commissioners to Patera, the next part of their journey, on 2nd January. Travelling round rural Wales, even crossing its many streams and rivers, wouldn't have prepared these men for some aspects of the river crossings.

One of the bridges was down and they all had to get out of the car while Les drove through the river. The men had to walk along a rough, bamboo footbridge and William Davies slipped and fell headlong into the river. It was not deep enough to be dangerous but he was soaked to the skin and he had to change everything there and then on the road, Les keeping off the curious passers-by.

Because there had been such open discussions between members of the Commission and the church leaders, recommended changes did not come as a surprise. The time had come for more power to be handed to the Indian church members. From now on, missionaries were to come under the authority of the churches, not vice versa, with missionaries' councils being done away with.

A letter to supporters in the middle of July reports the prayer that "all concerned in the working out of their recommendations may be truly led of God, that the fruit of their visit may be greater efficiency in the work and a consequent increase in the work." National politics had their echoes within some of the findings.

One thing that was very evident during their visit was the desire of the Indian Christians for a greater measure of control and authority in the work. All over India the voice of Nationalism is strongly heard. In national affairs it is poor comfort for the Indian that the British

Government is just and has greatly benefited the country. He feels much the same as a householder would feel if someone else broke into his house, seized the keys and started to run the household.

Of course for long-term mission workers some changes must have been painful, although it seems people took them calmly. The saintly Mr. Roberts comes in for special mention in this regard, especially over the closing of the hospital and school in Habiganj for which he was responsible.

As a footnote to the work of the Commission, it seems that four months of travelling around took a toll on their health. Mr. William Davies "developed tonsillitis and ran a high temperature for some days, causing great anxiety." Finally they got him to the hospital in Shillong, where he was described as "looking terribly washed out." Presumably his earlier fall into a river wouldn't have helped.

Leaving Maulvi Bazaar

In August 1936, two years after they had started in Maulvi Bazaar, came a letter from the committee in Liverpool announcing news of their transfer to Shangpung, which meant living in a very different environment. Their main reservation about moving to the hills seems to have been the language switch from Bengali. They would be back to basic communication until they knew some of the new language.

Today, we had a great bombshell in the shape of a letter from Liverpool notifying us that we are to be transferred to Shanpung, a remote station in the Jaintia Hills. We simply did not know what to think. At the beginning of the year the Commission were very keen that we should go to the Hills and asked if should be willing to do so, and we said yes. There were two possibilities, both of them allowing of some English work, which Les could do while he was learning Khasi, so that he would not have another period of being held up through not knowing the language. But, the committee at home turned down these proposals, because while the Commission was out here they had made other arrangements, and so we had practically given up thoughts of going to the hills, and have lately settled down to the prospect of staying here another two years. It is not therefore altogether a welcome proposal that we should be moved, and to a place where there is no English work, and Les will have to give the major portion of his time once again to learning a new language. We simply do not know what to think about it, and were too unsettled to do anything all day.

Two days later, and with the arrival of two more letters, they were feeling "somewhat encouraged" about the move to Shangpung, a village described as having about one fifth of the population as "genuinely Christian." One thing that turned the tide of their feelings was the belief that where they were on the Plains they were living like Europeans and therefore their message could have little impact on people's lives. Why should Indian evangelists go and live in the villages while they, the missionaries, lived in comfortable bungalows?

We both feel that by our present mode of life we can get nowhere in the evangelisation of the district. It is my personal conviction that while we live as foreigners, our message will have little meaning for the people. After all, it is the witness of the preacher's life, backing up his preaching, which gives his preaching significance for his hearers, and although God can doubtless use his Word alone for conversions, and does so occasionally, yet for the most part Christianity has been spread through the infection of Christ-filled lives, explained of course by the witness of preaching and personal testimony.

A letter sent to supporters in Wales in late 1936 sums up the end to their time in Maulvi Bazaar.

In August, we had word that we were to be transferred from Maulvi Bazaar to Shangpung in the Jaintia Hills. There followed a very busy time packing. On the last evening we had our farewell meeting in the form of a communion service. In the quiet of dusk we gathered round the Lord's Table and realised that the people we were leaving, and ourselves, were in His hands.

5

MISSION WORK ON THE PLAINS AND THE HILLS

This chapter interrupts the chronological account of my parents' lives, to give small insights into the work in various North East locations where Welsh missionaries lived. Like the rest of this book, this chapter does not attempt to be a complete story of the 1930s work, but rather a series of snapshots.

THE PLAINS OF SYLHET AND CACHAR

Maulvi Bazaar

In the last chapter we saw the work in Maulvi Bazaar through my parents' eyes. The following account, taken from 13 handwritten pages, is headed *A brief description of Maulvi Bazaar* and adds to those personal commentaries. The pages may have been prepared for them by a local Christian as an introduction to the district, or perhaps it was meant to be read by people higher up in the Mission's organisation. Could it even have been prepared for members of the 1936, Commission from Wales? Whoever its intended readership, one thing that makes the account interesting is that as well as being factual, it offers both criticisms and suggestions.

Overview of Sylhet District

First there is an overview of Sylhet District's population. Half a million people were spread over 1643 villages with a majority of Hindus and Muslims, but also including hill tribes and South Indians. Perhaps the latter were the tea plantation workers mentioned in my parents' letters.

The Christian population was only 791, living in 15 locations, some with an actual church (Maulvi Town, Jagchara, Chempera and Karimpur), others meeting as small groups, such as Madhabrur, 22 miles south of the town, where there were 12 believers. The writer, who is presumably a Christian, speaks very critically of the lack of Christian influence in the district and in particular the fact that no difference could be seen between the "social and spiritual life" of a Christian and a non-Christian. Christians are said to be lacking zeal for the Kingdom of God.

Production was rice, tea and jute. The writer notes that "the low and depressed classes" who depended on the right amount of rain for the paddy fields, suffered "unspeakable" miseries when they were unable to pay the rent because of flooding.

There is one civil hospital in the town and some branch hospitals in the villages. Every year hundreds of people die of cholera and malaria epidemics in the town and in the villages.

Another problem was misunderstandings of the relationship between missionaries and the British rulers. In the writer's words:

[People believe] the Christians are the spies of the British Government. If any spy (the preachers and the missionaries) can convert one non-Christian into the Christian religion (which is the Sahibs' religion) then that spy get hundreds of rupees from the British Government. The motive is this: that without the riches of India the British nation cannot prosper in this world.

Furthermore, the location of the Mission House in Maulvi Bazaar, which was intended to be the centre of activities, "is situated in a very inconvenient place," the nearest railway station being twelve miles away. That meant that in the rainy season it was impossible to visit many of the branch churches without a boat.

Christian Work in the Namasudra Villages

More positively, the "workers and missionaries" come in for some praise for their work amongst non-Christian groups, such as the 150 Namasudra villages in the subdivision. These are described as "low class people in the Hindu community," repressed by those of higher station, and not having access to education. Four areas of work are mentioned: advice to villagers about their everyday affairs, preaching the gospel, advice on getting out of their "misery and oppression," school visits for examining children's progress and telling Bible stories.

Only one of the teachers was a Christian. The writer's suggestion was to put in Christian teachers despite the cost of supplying them with living quarters and paying them more than the current rate of 3 to 7 rupees monthly. In seven of the schools listed the teachers were actually unpaid.

An annual gathering of Namasudra society had been going for a few years, with the goal of bringing them under the Christian influence. The writer concludes with an opinion about future projects, using this work as a model.

Much work has been done and much money has been spent for the town's rich people. If this money would have been spent for the villages then by this time there would be many Christians. The town establishments should be broken and put in the far-in villages and the work should be done properly as it used to be in the towns.

Sylhet

An account of work in Sylhet has already been given in Chapter 3 in the context of my parents' orientation time there.

Silchar

More than 100 miles east of Maulvi Bazaar was Silchar, where a mission school had first been opened in 1856.

Missionaries in Silchar

Mr. Adams, who was temporarily in charge of Silchar as well as Karimganj, was described as "looking terribly ill, a sort of grey colour." Then there were Miss Rees and Miss James who shared a bungalow. On one visit Miss Rees met them and drove them in her little Austin car up to the bungalow. The car also came into its own for a drive around the locality at speeds of between 20 and 30 miles an hour, which seemed fast to the passengers, especially in view of the crowds of people and animals on the road. That compared dramatically with their usual driving experience of covering the 14 mile Maulvi to Srimongol road in an hour.

On the Silchar compound was a large hostel for girls. There were pleasantly surprised to meet a 14 year old girl, an orphan, who had been taken to Wales once some years earlier and had sung at a Sunday School gathering. The hostel eating arrangements sound complicated. Hindu girls from different castes who couldn't eat together had separate meal arrangements, as did the Christian girls. In fact each group had its own cook house.

The Missions Girls' High School with 300 students was the largest on the Plains. It included a kindergarten and a Teachers' Training Class. Men were not entirely absent, though, because in each room a punkah wallah did his work.

1936 Assembly in Silchar

Silchar was the site of the 1936 Assembly, where the big news was about the organisational changes hinted at earlier by the Commissioners from Wales.

This Assembly is a very important one. It is the wish of the Commission to give the Indian church as much power as possible, and this coincides with the coming to a head of agitation for this same thing that has been going on for some time, apparently, amongst the Indians. There has been much discussion at the Assembly this year and at last a very momentous decision arrived at: that the missionaries are to come under the authority of the church, the missionaries' councils being done away with and a committee, consisting of Indians and Europeans, is to manage all the work.

Of course this move reflected changes in India as a whole, changes that had not come quickly. The Indian National Congress, founded as early as 1885, had developed a nationalist wing and before the end of World War One the call had come for home rule. Gradual steps had been taken, spurred on by Gandhi's non-violent protests and the more radical approach of Jawaharlal Nehru, later to be Prime Minister. In 1935, just before this latest Assembly, the Government of India Act had given Indians full autonomy at the provincial level. Changes in the mission work were part of that move.

As reported earlier in her letters my mother was sympathetic to the changes, saying that *"the leaders of the church no longer wish to be in the position of children dependent upon a missionary, however benevolent a 'father' he may be. At the same time, many of the 'rank and file,' particularly of the evangelists, continue in the old attitude towards the missionary, looking upon him as their security, material and otherwise. The question of the independence of the Indian Church is complicated by the poverty of many of the lay members of the church, especially compared with the standard of living that is generally considered desirable for the ministry. This means that the church cannot support its own workers without great sacrifice on the part both of members, in respect to giving, and workers, in respect to receiving. There would be some relief to this problem if there could be a bigger proportion of converts from the middle and upper classes, who would be able to contribute more liberally towards the expenses of the work than the majority of members are able to do at present. There are regrettably few members of the church of this class apart from those in mission employ. You may think that these questions of organisation and finance are far removed from the simple preaching of the Gospel which is our real business. That is true, and yet these things hold such a prominent place just now in the thoughts and feelings of the people concerned that sometimes there is a danger lest preaching be hindered, and it is of much importance that the organisation of the church be such as to conduce to the building of a strong church.*

Another change which emerged during the Silchar Assembly, but which did not directly affect my parents, was that the four Mission schools should be closed now that the government was "awake to the need for education."

Karimganj

The Karimganj district was described by Morris (1930: 72-3) as having 600 Namasudra boys and 300 girls in schools in 1911. By my parents' time Rev. and Mrs. Adams were in charge and plans were on hold for Miss Hetty Evans to be transferred there. Work with the Namasudra villagers has already been described.

Habiganj

The Habiganj Subdivision was extensive, with 2,500 villages (Morris, 1930: 74). Christian work there had been handed back to the Welsh Presbyterian Mission in 1922 by the American churches. The buildings included a hospital for women and a girls' School although, as noted, one of the recommendations of the 1936 Commission from Wales, was to close down the school and hospital.

The district's reputation for terrorism and dacoits must have made things difficult for the two single missionary women. Blodwen Williams was the teacher substituting during Elsie Andrew's furlough and Winnie Thomas was in charge of the hospital in the absence of Lilian Payne. Driving to Habiganj to visit these two from time to time was described by my parents as a pleasant duty, although the word 'pleasant' didn't always describe the journey.

On one occasion my father, who had started to learn to drive after they went to Maulvi Bazaar, took the wheel for the whole 45 miles along a difficult road including river crossings, some by bridge and some by ferry. On the other side, he nearly drove into the river but with men pushing the car up the bank, all was well. Not surprisingly, Mofus Babu drove on the way home in the dark. My mother describes herself as also being a learner driver "though I am terribly clumsy about it, and I do not think I shall ever make a really good driver." She must have let those skills lie dormant for some years, because one of my childhood memories is of sitting in the back seat while my father gave her driving lessons along country roads in the South Island of New Zealand.

At one point my parents were to be moved to Habiganj. An issue that concerned my parents was the size of missionary bungalows there, much larger than the dwellings of the evangelists. If a move happened they were determined not to have a bungalow built for them. "It would be a negation of all we came out for." That worry was removed by a fire. On Monday 18th February, 1935 a telegram announced, "BASHA BURNT NOTHING LEFT." Basha was the name of the house they were to have lived in. Still, they set off the following month for their planned visit, staying in Shaistaganj but visiting the site of the fire 40 minutes away in Habiganj.

Their hostess, Miss Evans, had a system of bringing new village converts in to the town for a while to give them Christian training. One new Christian who was baptised in Habiganj had some standing in the town. He was the "principal of quite an important Hindu college" and had come to Will Morgan asking for baptism, which was a big step for someone in that position.

The great risk is that the college authorities will tell him that they no longer require his services (April 1936). It was interesting to read of this conversion in the light of the earlier reflection on the absence of professional people amongst Christian converts.

Presbytery Meeting in Habiganj

Another time they made the journey to Habiganj by a combination of car and train for a November Presbytery meeting, leaving Shanwah in charge at Maulvi Bazaar. The train ride gave rise to a social dilemma. Of the four classes, they were travelling by second class and their friend and colleague Mr. Ghose by intermediate (one step below). They solved the problem by having him with them for the first half of the journey and then travelling with him for the second half.

One of the Indian speakers at the Presbytery was from Calcutta, where he worked for the CPSSM. He spoke to the children using "the very latest in method." Perhaps it was because he was addressing children that my mother could follow the Bengali of his message. She herself also had to give her talk in Bengali.

My father, too, had a turn at speaking, but to a different audience.

In the evening Les gave an English lecture in the Town Hall. All the professional men of the town as well as many others turned up, although this is so nationalistic a place and the chairman (by Miss Evans' invitation) was one of the leaders in the anti-British movement. I thought it very remarkable to perform this office.....

The Life of New Christians

They heard one more example of what it was like to choose to become a Christian from a different faith background.

There is a Hindu living in the town, who went to Miss Evans a little while ago and told her that his father used to read the New Testament regularly and taught him to do so. With his father's death he lost his most valued friend and came to love Jesus, until this was now the chief thing in his life. His own people could not understand all his emotions and he felt that he would like to speak of all that was bottled up within him to the Christians. Miss Evans of course agreed and he spoke in a church meeting and again in a meeting of the presbytery.

On another occasion (the Haflong meetings in late 1936), a crisis in Habiganj interrupted proceedings. Will Morgan had been called back suddenly from the meetings. When he reached Kaluara by train he was met by one of the evangelists from Habiganj with an urgent request to return there immediately.

The new convert, Mr. Dey has had a sudden collapse and it was feared that he would not last the night. We were all very upset about it. He has had a terrible persecution. They even took away his cook from him, and he is a delicate man suffering from pernicious anaemia. Will suspects that his collapse is due to foul play, though I don't suppose there will ever be any proof of that.....Mr. Dey has no friends left now, but just the missionaries, so they cannot leave him at this crisis.

Will returned to Habiganj, having spent all night on the train. It seemed that the two women missionaries from there chose to stay behind too, rather than travelling to the Haflong meeting.

Haflong

Haflong was the Government headquarters in that part of the Hills. In late 1936, my parents went there for the District Commission. They met again met the Harries Rees couple, who had been in India since 1912, having first seen them when the couple passed through Sylhet at the end of 1933. The wife was described as looking "wonderfully well and young" while he had been very ill with cerebral malaria. Morris mentions that they had been helping with the translation of the Gospel of Mark in 1929.

Shaistaganj

From time to time my parents met someone who gave them a fresh insight into what it meant to give a lifetime of service to another country. During a meeting in Habiganj it was Miss Laura Evans of Shaistaganj whose life impresses them, especially in relation to what happens to people in old age.

She really is a marvel. I think that she is at least seventy and she lives all alone. She has been out for many, many years and still seems to be working with unflagging energy. She is such a little, shrivelled looking person, and the word that comes to mind in thinking of her is heroic. All through this Presbytery she worked hard, attending every meeting. Her furlough is long due, but she is not taking it. She has few friends left at home now and none of her own people. Also, it seems, she is afraid that if she went home the committee might make her retire.

Difficulties for local people are also mentioned. In the following instance, it is interesting to note that a telegram was worded in Welsh for security reasons.

After tea an urgent telegram came from Shaistaganj, where Miss Laura Evans is, asking Mr. Roberts to go there at once. In a village near the station a Mohammedan convert is being severely persecuted. He dare not move out of the house because the Mohammedans threaten to kill him. One day a spear was thrust through the wall of the house and would have killed him had not a piece of wood intervened. The trouble is now spreading and threatens to affect the whole Christian community. Miss Evans was very concerned when she was here this week and her telegram, which had to be in Welsh, says that things are worse. I think she is very brave. She is the only European living in the place and is almost elderly, yet she sticks it and does a wonderful work and is much respected in the district. The convert concerns shows no signs of yielding but this sort of thing helps one to understand why converts are so few. Apart from the danger to his life, this man is boycotted and will soon be reduced to poverty.

Patera

Patera (or Bhatera) was 20 miles from Sylhet and the site of a Theological College for training Indian evangelists. In my parents' time the principal was Mr. Hridesh Ghose who had previously been principal of the Boys' School in Sylhet, as well as being an evangelist. As we saw from their time in Maulvi Bazaar, my parents had a close relationship with him. He was the one who had helped my mother prepare for her Bengali examination in Calcutta, and later, in March 1935 he had asked if my mother would teach Greek to one of his sons. Therefore, the sad news that reached them in February 1936 was a personal blow.

Just when we were writing our mail a wire came with the utterly unexpected news that Mrs. Ghose of Bhatera was dead and was to be buried at twelve that day. … Everybody was very shocked, and there were hasty preparations to go to Bhatera in time for the funeral-all the men with Les in the car, immediately after breakfast. They arrived there at ten to twelve but it had been found necessary to have the funeral earlier, so they were not in time for that.

Mrs Ghose had died absolutely suddenly, with not so much as five minutes' notice. Mr. Ghose had returned Sunday morning from Calcutta where he had been attending special meetings and Mrs Ghose was quite alright. The boys were in Sylhet sitting their annual exams and they two were alone when suddenly at 7.30 p.m. Mrs Ghose said, "I'm going." Then "God forgive my sins" and she was gone.

THE KHASI HILLS

Shillong

My parents were in Shillong a number of times, sometimes for mission-related work and at other times for a holiday at the end of the hot season. The usual practice for holidays was to stay for a month in a mission bungalow built for visitors, leaving just as the rains were about to break. There they would meet other missionaries and hear about work in various parts of the North East.

Synod Meetings

When they were there for meetings, the arrangements were different. For one of the Synods they were accommodated at the hospital, staying in the doctor's quarters. They said they didn't mind at all having to be quiet in the afternoons and evenings.

The Synod meetings involved huge gatherings, such as those held one late October in English and in Khasi.

The services were held in the open air, and crowds attended. It is always an inspiring sight to see literally thousands gathered on the grass. People were asking questions. ..... One thing that pleases Mr. Pugh (who is in charge of the church) is the fact that old boys of the school who have left for college and various posts, always attend the service when they are in Shillong.

Mr. Pugh

Mr. Pugh had resigned from the staff of the City of Cardiff High School for Boys to be principal of the government school and was also in charge of a big hostel for boys in the hills.

Mr. Pugh and Students in Shillong, Sept. 1934

Apparently "every single one of them attended his Bible Class, even though it was voluntary." There is reference to Mr. Pugh's little daughter Enid who was back in Britain.

Dr. Gordon Roberts

Dr. Roberts, head of the Mission Hospital, was mentioned earlier as having raised the money to build it when my mother was a child. He and his wife were living there. During a hospital visit my parents talked with a Bengali maternity patient who had nobody to speak to in her language. Either their language had made progress by then, or the woman was good at making the most of a few words.

Mr. Harries Rees

One Sunday afternoon they went to what they described as the English church, attended by European officials, missionaries, and schoolboys wearing tribal costumes. My father was the preacher that day. The multilingual nature of North East India shows in a reference to another sermon being given three times over, each time in a different tongue. Mr. Harries Rees, who preached all three, must have had considerable language talents.

Annie Thomas and Hilda Jones

On the visit mentioned in Chapter 4, my father stayed in with malaria, for which the treatment seemed to be bedrest plus quinine, which left the patient with a bad headache. My mother carried on with some of the organised programme, which included lunch with Miss Annie Thomas who did evangelistic and literary work and with Miss Hilda Jones, headmistress of the Girls' High School. However, in the interests of looking after the patient she missed the visit to Mawphlang, 15 miles away to see Rev. and Mrs. Gwillym Jones.

Visitors from Nagaland

In Shillong my parents first met people from Nagaland who were described as amongst the first Christians and suffering persecution from the tribal leaders. They had brought with them a woman who had recently become a Christian and had obtained permission from the headman of the village to move to a Christian village.

Christians had formed villages of their own, where they may follow their own practices instead of having to join in these heathen feasts. The headmen have a way of granting permission to a convert to leave the village, then as soon as they have settled down they pretend they have not given permission, and appeal to the district magistrate to punish the 'offender.'

Cherrapunji

During a September 1934 visit to Shillong they went to Cherrapunji (Sohra) where they saw the remains of the mission buildings destroyed by an earthquake in the 1880s. The ruins were still there but the rebuild had been done further away. The amazing views impressed them, as they did me eighty years later when I went with a group of NECTAR students. They saw a deep gorge with "the longest waterfall in the world" and reported seeing as far as the college at Sylhet, nearly 100 miles away. The air must have been clearer on that day than during my visit, when Cherrapunji was demonstrating its reputation for wetness. Apart from its physical beauty, Cherrapunji had special memories for the church. Gibbard (2004) recalls that it was the site of the February 1905 Assembly, where Dr. Roberts gave news of the Welsh Revival.

At the College they saw its "fine library" where a service was held in which the students "took part very heartily in the singing." They expressed the hope that Mr. Evans, then in his late seventies, would be spared for many years' service since he was such an excellent missionary.

Besides the college he has a very large and difficult district to work. It is very hilly and touring involves climbing up and down paths so rough and steep that a pony is impossible and he has to do it all on foot. …. He looks such a frail man yet he does all this and is a fine walker.

There was also a Middle English school at Cherrapunji with hostels "and very occasionally someone will proceed to the High School at Shillong."

At a village school they photographed the children.

September 1934 Group of Children at Cherrapunji

Mawphlang

During one visit to Shillong my parents were taken to visit the work in Mawphlang. Basil Griffiths (2007) gives a detailed account of his grandfather's medical work there 120 years earlier and paints a picture of a dispensary still operating at the time of his own 21st century visit.

THE JAINTIA HILLS

The work at Shangpung and Jowai is described in Chapters 6 and 7.

THE LUSHAI HILLS

There is less in my parents' letters about the work in the Lushai Hills, but a thorough account appears in Meirion Lloyd's (1952) book. He refers to the work of Katie Hughes, whom my parents had first met in Calcutta when her children's choir was touring. Her work with children included a child welfare clinic in Aijal and the training of Sunday School teachers.

In March 1938, it was time for the Lushai Assembly to be held at Latkynsew which, as it turned out would be my parents' last. The Synod nearly didn't happen because of floods. News of rumblings in Europe started to reach them too. In fact the two questions people had asked them earlier in Shillong were these. "Do you know there is probably going to be war? Have you heard about the floods and Lushai?" One of these predictions proved wrong, and the synod went ahead with some very encouraging news. An interesting new mission development was discussed, involving an initiative by the Lushais

The Lushais are starting an interesting new piece of work. They are going to run their own 'foreign' mission in a frontier tract, and Mr. Mendus has been asked to approach the governor for permission to open the work. The government official who is over the reserved areas ... is very much against missions, therefore it was doubtful whether permission would be given, but Mr. Mendus was very pleased to find that the governor himself is very favourably impressed by the project, so there is hope.

6

SHANGPUNG

The Journey to Shangpung

We have been hearing a great deal about Shangpung. Everybody thinks we shall be very happy there and that it is the right thing for Les to have the opportunities for preaching which work on the hills affords.... It is three days' journey from Shillong (along jungle tracks, on foot or by pony...)....

It is one of the largest districts in the hills, there being something like 150 schools and churches. There is a great deal of touring to be done, all on horseback (16th Aug., 1936).

So off They Went

It is 33 miles to Jowai, and for the first three miles there is a motor road. Mr. Roberts, with his usual generosity, has offered to drive us to the end of this road.

From there on there were various options: walking, horse riding or being carried in a basket.

We soon arrived at the end of the motor road, mounted our steeds, had a snap taken and rode off. We have four horses and one topper (a basket on a man's back, in which one can be carried). They said at first that one of the men had better ride my horse, as it was new and we did not know how it would behave, but anyway, they put me on it and actually let me go off first on my own......

Our first day's journey was 14 miles, and we did it partly walking, partly riding.

The Crossing Over the Kapili River

The scenery impressed them, with its wooded hills, its valleys and its rivers. The pattern was to walk down and ride up. Finally they reached the dak bungalow where they were to spend the night, sharing the space, as it turned out, with two Catholic nuns.

Next day the distance was 16 miles, partly through open land with no shade and therefore quite hot. Despite mention of baskets for carrying humans, it seems that one member of the party, Miss Buckley, was too heavy to be carried and therefore spent most of the day on horseback. My mother's reason for choosing never to be carried "unless it is absolutely necessary" was to do with her feelings of having one human carry another. Soon the town of Jowai was close.

At about 3 o'clock we reached the last valley, climbed down the steep hill, walked across the bottom then mounted our horses for the last climb up. The scenery was really wonderful; I had not imagined it would be so beautiful.

For the final 13 miles of the journey to Shangpung they had to wait for a fine day. When that happened on October the 8th off they went, reaching the village at sunset where a number of people were waiting to welcome them.

In dry weather there was a "shorter" route between Jowai and Shangpung, although one mile seems hardly to qualify for the word. When they had to return to Jowai the following month they decided to take this "shortcut" since the rains had stopped enough to make it passable. They wondered whether, although shorter, it really was quicker or not.

We had to climb down a steep hill and clamber over boulders and jump streams at the bottom. One stream was too wide to jump, so we had to take turns to cross it on Duke. Then came some fields and then another ride across the river. I went first and Duke thought he would enjoy himself in the water by pawing it and incidentally soaking my feet and legs. Then we had to scramble up steep rocks dodging the stream and the waterfalls......

Over their months in Shangpung they visited Jowai more than once. A journey in November, 1936 gave them an unexpected and dramatic view which was captured in poetic language in the daily journal.

Just before the 8th mile (from Jowai) I was sitting on the horse and happened to turn my head to the right to drink in all the beauty of the *morning, when I espied the snows away in the distance... a long line of snows against the blue sky. We could hardly believe our eyes. They must have been getting on for two hundred miles away, for in between were the rest of these hills then the whole width of the Upper Assam (Brahmaputra) Valley, then the lower Himalayas. We just feasted our eyes on the view and then caught it again several times before reaching the 6th mile.*

Discovering Shangpung

The next part of their life started in October 1936. They met Nondw the cook and Kron, the woman who would do the cleaning. Her language was Khasi, which must have made things difficult until my parents learned the language. Kron's husband Ho would be the sais (looking after the horses) and also attend to the garden. Although, they weren't to know it then, their stay in the village would be relatively short.

On their first day they strolled to a nearby non-Christian village. Maybe strolled is an understatement because the path led through a deep ravine with tall jungle on both sides. On their first Sunday they met in the large church, which was full of people for the 10 a.m. service. Next came the women's meeting to which people brought bags of rice for the Rice Collection which supported schools amongst other projects. One o'clock was their welcome meeting, combined with a farewell for the Jones couple.

The photograph shows their bungalow and its beautiful garden with rose bushes, dahlias, hydrangeas and over the verandah a flowing bougainvillea. A lawn led down to tall fir trees. A vegetable garden and an orchard added to the appeal.

Their initial impressions were summarised in a letter to supporters in Wales.

Coming here was quite a new experience for us. There are no trains and no motor roads, so it took us three days to reach here from Shillong, walking and riding. Now we have to start on the language once again. Khasi is used for the services and is understood by all but the very ignorant, but the local dialect – Paar-is different. It felt very strange at the beginning not to be able to speak to anybody, especially as the school had broken up for the autumn holiday, so the people who know English were nearly all away.

There are eight classes in the school, from infants up to Class 6. Pupils from the top class sit for the Middle English examination, which gives entrance to the high school at Shillong. Boys and girls come from all parts of the district-some have several days' journey to reach here-and stay in the hostels.

There is also a mission dispensary. The empounder who is in charge has been ill since we have been here, so we have had to see all the patients who come. It is quite difficult to understand what is wrong with them when we cannot understand their language, but the work is interesting. Besides giving out medicine from the dispensary, we also had calls to visit the sick in their houses, and thus get to know the people.

When next we write we hope to have more news to give of our new work. Meanwhile we wish all our friends a Christmas season of great joy, and God's richest blessing for the New Year.

Yours in the bonds of His service,
W. L. and W. B. Lewis

Because of the isolation of the district, one of my father's regular responsibilities was to pay people and to give medicine as needed. These processes were spread out, rather than happening on a specific day, which meant he had time to talk with people and get to know them. That was the part he enjoyed.

Some live so far away that they come only once every three months. One man came yesterday, a pastor from the border and he had walked through the jungle where he had seen many bears and other wild beasts.

Other, sadder events could come unexpectedly, such as the sudden death of a three year old girl living opposite their bungalow, the only child of one of the teachers. She had made an impression on them soon after their arrival.

The second day we were here they called on us and the little girl sang to us. I thought what a nice little family they were.

A cough she had for a week developed into a fever and then she was gone. At the funeral there was of course much weeping.

Unexpected visitors called in from time to time, such as the S.D.O. who was in tour in November, 1936. He turned out to be a Khasi Christian.

Church Life

Church life in Shangpung impressed them from the start.

The church in Shangpung was strong, with good sized congregations each Sunday... The Welsh Revival at the start of the century had leapt the oceans and taken over in the Welsh mission fields in India, so that even after the effects became weak in Wales, they continued to strengthen in the Khasi Hills.

There are no pastors or evangelists in Shangpung but two of the ordinary members of the church or young teachers from the district preach every Sunday.

Of the four deacons, two are young men; the precentor is young, also the Superintendent of the Sunday School, and of the children's meeting. Young people take part freely in the meetings and even preach.

There is quite a large church here, and a school with a hostel each for boys and girls. The meetings are held on the lines of meetings in Welsh churches at home-the weeknight meeting is in the form of a 'seiat' and so on. Sunday is a very full day: it starts with a prayer meeting at 7 a.m., Sunday School at 10, followed immediately by the Women's Meeting, preaching services at one and at three, Children's Meeting at 4.30. Meals have to be squeezed in as best we can-several times we have been in the middle of a meal when the bell has gone and we have had to rush off. It seems that the people are unwilling to reduce the number of meetings, for fear that the young people would go out walking!

There were special meetings for New Year 1937, the first early in the morning and another at about one o'clock, each signalled by the ringing of the church bell.

There was no sermon but one of the deacons spoke and at the end they had a thanksgiving offering, everybody coming forward and laying their offerings on the table. Even the little children in their mothers' arms (it would be more correct to say 'on their backs') held pice which their mothers told them to place on the table. I noticed one or two silently offer a prayer before walking back.

The day continued with two more gatherings, one at three and another, a prayer meeting, in the evening.

The School and Hostel

The school was described as Middle English, starting with infants and going going up to high school entrance at about 14 years of age. The headmaster was newly out from college and had a degree and as well there were other teachers. English was taught in four classes.

In the school also the teachers appear to be under thirty, and the headmaster has but lately left college.

A girls' hostel on the compound was just behind the bungalow. My mother looked forward to working with the eight girls who are photographed here in March, 1937.

Touring the District

Occasionally their visits beyond the village were close enough to walk.

Today we visited a church only about three miles away-a very pleasant walk.

Travel to further parts of the district was sometimes by boat and often on horseback, but the first problem was finding the right horses.

We haven't been able to find a horse large enough for Les yet. The problem is to get one light enough for the climbing and heavy enough to carry 14 st. (October 1936)

The photograph album shows them visiting other villages, such as Kairang and Sutnga in November and December 1937.

Church at Bataw

District tour November, December 1937

Photos of their District tour of November, December 1937

7

JOWAI

As we have seen, moving from station to station was a feature of the Welsh missionaries' lives. After only six months in Shangpung they were transferred again, this time to Jowai, the chief town of the Jaintia Hills. They arrived on Friday 23rd July 1937 to replace Rev. Gwilym Jones and his wife Helen who were going home on furlough. The Jones couple too had done their share of moving, worked first on the Plains from 1924, then in Lushai before moving to Jowai.

The Setting of Jowai

Before we come to the personal news from the diaries and letters, here is some information about the district written locally at the time. There are ten typed and unsigned pages tied together with string and a couple of metal pieces which have left rust marks over the years. Although, like the earlier notes about Maulvi Bazaar, they are anonymous, undated and their intended readership is not mentioned, their account seems worth mentioning as part of the district's history. Mention of the most recent census as being in 1931 is the only clue to their date. Here is a combination of quotes and summaries, starting with some history.

The area had come into British rule about a century earlier (1835) when its Raja, Indra Singh, was deposed, but by 1862 all was not well between locals and the British.

In 1860 when a house tax was imposed on the Phars an outbreak of disaffection to the British rule took place and in 1862 a serious outbreak occurred when the Police station in Jowai was razed to the ground, the garrison of sepoys was besieged and all show of British authority was swept away throughout the Hills.

A Colonel Dunsford had managed to restore peace by the following year.

We are also told about the population and geography.

The area of the Jowai Subdivision, or as it is commonly known, the Jaintia Hills, is 2106 square miles. There are 776 villages… with about 15740 occupied houses.

These were the population figures:

Males 39, 144 Females 42, 001 TOTAL 81, 145

The Jowai Subdivision is bounded on the north by the Nowgong District, on the east by the Kopili River and the Cachar District, on the south by the Sylhet District and on the west by the Khasi Hills.

The subdivision was almost entirely made up of hills, with only the occasional patches of low lying land. Jowai, the headquarters, was 4,500 feet above sea level. The higher ranges the hills had been denuded of trees in favour of grass, longer in the lower areas, shorter higher up. There were reasons why some trees were left in place.

A remarkable feature… throughout the hills, is the numerous sacred groves, which superstition has preserved from the destructive hand of the woodcutter. These sacred groves contain beautiful timber trees of various kinds, rare orchids and ferns.

The ground was granite and sandstone, limestone and shale with coal beds and morphic rocks. Amongst the many caves and caverns the writer mentions the most notable as "the cave at Rumpath is Satpator doloiship." The higher part had no roads or navigable rivers but down towards the Plains of Sylhet the large streams allowed for small boats or canoes for short distances between rapids.

The Mission

We now return to my parents' account. Jowai was familiar to them from several visits during their stay in Shangpung, sometimes for meetings or for medical reasons such as having anti-typhoid injections soon after moving to the hills. People there used two languages: Bengali with educated Indians and Khasi, the tribal language which was also the language of their Bible. The written form of the Khasi language had been developed by earlier Welsh missionaries.

The missionary bungalow was on one of the two Jowai Hills, along with the church and the hospital. Below them was the middle school and at the foot there was the town.

Helen Jones initiated my mother into the school work that she would be overseeing.

The missionary's wife acts as superintendent of the school, takes sewing in the top class for the exam, and supervises all the work, advising the teachers and taking lessons where she considers that necessary. Other regular tasks are speaking at a weekly meeting in the heathen village, looking after the girls' hostel … , keeping various accounts in connection with the women's work, taking a Sunday School class, the women's meeting and the children's meeting.

It wasn't a surprise to read that the part my mother dreaded was the sewing class, including cutting out garments without a pattern. Throughout our childhood she did what was needed for sewing and knitting our clothes, but she much preferred reading to us. In between more formal duties in Jowai there was the task of caring for the hens which were the source of fresh eggs.

There was an interesting insight into the how and why of Sunday observance in Jowai.

It is the custom here to fill every possible minute of Sundays with meetings. The Jones have tried to get them to leave one out, but they refuse, on the grounds that the young people would walk out in the roads. So, they start at 6.30 a.m. and go on all day, and the poor children have to sit through all those.

Touring Beyond the Town

As in Maulvi Bazaar, work extended beyond the town. There was a fair bit of travelling around the villages during the cold season.

Touring meant going round visiting all the Christian schools in the villages. These were the same teachers that we saw each month when they came to get their pay. In every village they would have prepared by building a grass hut for us to spend the night. The routine was to reach the village before nightfall, meet the teacher and have a church service, because the teacher would act as the pastor, and this was his chance to confer with the missionaries over any problems. Then next morning you'd inspect the school. The missionary was meant to ask the children questions. Les was a bit unconventional. He asked questions like "What's the point of a cow's tail?" which weren't on the syllabus.

They had an introduction to work in the villages on their first Sunday before the Jones couple left, although that was a short journey.

Gwylim had to go to a village [Demtring] five miles away to give communion, so we all decided to go with him. We had to descend right down to the river, then climb a very steep hill.... They built a new church only a couple of years ago, and it was really quite a nice building.

The description of the congregation and the service shows why Rev. Jones had so much enjoyed going out to work in the villages. Most of the 50 women present had nursing babies and there were also older toddlers plus older girls sitting in the middle between the women and the men and boys, who sat on the other side.

In late 1937 their touring took them further afield, as my mother recalled sixty years later (Lewis, 1996:138-9).

One year instead of the usual tour we did something else. On the eastern border of Jaintia was the territory of the Cachar Hills where another couple worked in the capital, Haflong. We decided to meet on our border and after a weekend there to trek back towards Jowai, a journey of several days. First we crossed the river. I have photos showing us standing two at a time on the flimsy rafts being propelled across by the driver, the two men on one raft, the women on another, and the coolies on a third with our luggage. In the background are the horses, who had to swim across. The villages where we spent the nights had two grass huts built for the two couples.

Some rivers we crossed on bamboo bridges which were far from level, and high up from the water. There were no such things as handrails, so crossing them was quite a balancing feat. Once when the horses refused to cross, the sais had to lead them down to the water for them to swim across the rocky river. At the end of a memorable journey our friends then spent Christmas with us in our Jowai bungalow.

That was the Harries Rhys couple. A photograph shows him honouring the occasion by appearing at the breakfast table on Christmas Day wearing a dog collar.

Hospital Work

From Morris (1930) we have some background to the medical work started by Dr. Edward Williams who had first arrived in Jowai in 1893 to succeed Dr. A. D. Hughes. The building being used as a hospital in the 1930s had been planned by Dr. Williams only for outpatients although it had gone beyond that function and had its own doctor, an Indian employed by the Mission.

By the late 1930s Miss Buckley had been there for two years doing hospital work. As my parents moved around the building, they saw some of the patients she cared for. One seven year old boy, a cow herd, had been mauled by a tiger. Another boy, who was impaled by a stick when he fell off a tree, had been carried for several days to reach the hospital. They also saw, above each bed, a plaque with the name of the sponsoring church in Wales.

Fortunately for patients and staff, there were plans to upgrade, or rather to rebuild, the hospital. In October 1936, when approval had come through from Wales, "Messrs Roberts and Harries Rees [were] going there to choose a site for the new hospital."

I think Mr. Roberts must have been very tired and stiff, seeing that he is not accustomed to riding, and has been living in the enervating climate of the Plains for so long, but he was cheerful despite that. We were supposed to be going to see the possible sites for the hospital after tea, but it rained heavily, so they had to content themselves with discussing plans for the building.

The planning went on even while they were waiting for the weather to clear.

We have plenty of languages on the go in the house. Everybody except myself knows Welsh, and all except Miss Buckley use it habitually.... In addition to that, Khasi phrases naturally come in from time to time when appropriate. Three of us know Bengali, two know Hindustani..... one knows Lushai, four know a couple of dialects other than the main languages.

Once the rain stopped they could move ahead with inspecting possible sites.

The choice practically lies between two sites. One fronts right onto the main road of the town, next door to the Post Office, and runs back along a narrow ridge. The other is just beyond it. Miss Buckley favours the other site, because

It is convenient for the town people and also for combining house-to-house visiting with the hospital work.

Everyone else favours the other site, because it is larger, more open and in every way a better site but for the objection of distance. It is only about 100 yards further but involves rather a steep climb and considerable outlay on a road.

Selecting a suitable site included concerns about a water supply.

One great difficulty that has to be faced is the question of water. In a country where for several months of the year there is no rain this is a most serious problem. We had brought the horses out with us so that we could explore for a likely source of water.

Everyone took a break that afternoon except for the tireless Mr. Roberts.

He is very keen when there is a job like this going and is very good at it too. This is the third hospital that he has helped to plan and one of these he built also.

A day or two later came a hitch in the chosen site. When it came time to match the plans to the space available they discovered a dip in the ground.

By December, 1938 the old hospital was still in use. The Civil Surgeon, Major Haythornthwaite, had travelled 17 miles that day to do his regular inspection but wasted no time before starting on his duties. His visit was not just a formality since "our doctor can only do minor operations and one or two others, so major operations are done only when the C.S. comes on his annual visit."

Jowai Hospital at Christmas 1938

In January 1939 plans for the new hospital took a step forward.

The mission has decided to ask Dr. Lyngdoh, a Khasi Christian who has recently retired from government service, to take charge of the hospital here.

This doctor arrived for a preliminary visit while my parents were still there. Recalling their original three day journey to Shangpung, no wonder they were impressed that he had ridden from Shillong to Jowai in one day.

Furlough Postponed

The plan had been for the Jones couple to return to Jowai in late 1938, allowing my parents to return for furlough as was the custom, after five years in India. In September they were preparing to travel to Shillong for committees and then to Lushai for the Synod, then back to Shillong for the S.C. after which they would return to Jowai to pack for their furlough. However, a letter arrived from Gwylim mentioning severe health issues which would prevent his returning in the near future, if at all. This meant a postponed furlough for my parents although, as events in Europe were unfolding, it soon seemed that nobody would be travelling anywhere by ship if war could not be averted.

They did go to Shillong as planned, and there, between meetings, this situation in Europe was at the top of people's concerns. International news seemed to trickle through gradually, depending on who had radio access at any particular time.

All the talk was of war. The doctor's own wireless was in Calcutta being repaired, so he is trying to hire one so as to get the news this week.

Even hiring a radio seemed a problem. The doctor's electricity supply was private, different from the town supply "so that cannot be used with most of the machines available."

In face of the war rumours my parents were told "that we probably will not be able to get home now, perhaps for years." People were cancelling their passages and even talking of bringing their children from British boarding schools to the safety of India. However, getting reliable up-to-date news from Europe seemed difficult.

Meanwhile everyone gathers each evening at Mr. Williams' to listen to his wireless, which isn't always as clear as it might be. Owing to committees this week there is quite a crowd of us here.

Different topics were occupying local people. People returning from one of the committee sessions just avoided bursts of fighting in the town. The cause was a Khasi political meeting that had been attended by some Congress people although "most of the Khasis are anti-Congress." My mother noted the irony of foreigners worrying about events in Munich while people around them had other concerns.

People are feeling a little better today because of news of the conference at Munich. Everybody is going round telling everybody else bits of news and various details concerning precautions at home, until things are becoming quite a strain. I suppose one can't help talking about it, but it all seems quite strange when we have just come from a world where the state of the rice crop is the one matter of concern for one's neighbours.

Fortunately some Europeans were carrying on with local projects, including the wife of the Civil Surgeon.

Mrs. Haythornthwaite had very kindly invited us to coffee at the Assam Industries this morning. This is a shop run voluntarily by the lady members of the European community for the sale of goods made in Assam, and there is a coffee room attached.

On the last day of September 1938 came the European news people had been hoping for.

This morning everybody gathered at 7 a.m. to hear the result of the Munich conference. Great was the jubilation at the news of peace (Friday, 30th September).

That news seemed to free people to carry on as usual. Next day they went out to Mawphlang with Dr. Roberts, whose custom was to visit there each Saturday afternoon. Mrs. Roberts' health was such that unless it improved she would have to leave India. Part of her recovery process was a plan to spend all day in the mountains round Shillong, a plan for which she bought a new car, a Vauxhall 10.

Meanwhile my mother made a visit back to Jowai.

Menna, the newest of the three nurses came out with me to Jowai to get the things necessary for staying in Cartrefle [the mission house] and to give her a little change (3rd October).

Goodbye to India

Back in Jowai December was a busy month. As well as leading up to Christmas it was the examination month for the students. Children came from villages round about, carrying their sleeping gear, even ten year old primary school children. Before they left at the end of January 1939, messages home made it clear that they were expecting to return for a second term.

They spent the month of January on what they assumed would be temporary farewells. On Sunday 8th they travelled to the village of Nongbah, eight miles from Jowai for a district meeting. The reason they had never been there before was that the village had a pastor of their own there. In the middle of the month they went to Shangpung one last time. One highlight of the visit was that "Olly, Tell and Celmos were to be received into church membership and Tell's baby [was] to be christened."

Footnote

My parents returned to Wales where, by the end of the war they had three children and a parish in Neath. With India preparing for Independence our family sailed to New Zealand. My father had only five years there before he died of cancer. My mother lived on for another half century, raising her children, teaching, and leading church study groups.

REFERENCES

Almost all the original material for this book comes from the typed letters and diaries mentioned in the introduction. In addition, there are the two sets of anonymous notes mentioned in the text, one handwritten about Maulvi Bazaar and the other typed, giving information about Jowai. One further source was my mother's autobiography, dictated to me in her late eighties.

Lewis, Winifred (1996). *I Remember, I Remember.* Auckland (privately published).

I have also read an been inspired by the following books.

Barraclough, Geoffrey (1993 edition). *The Times History of the World.* London: Times Books.

Fielder, Geraint (1983). *Excuse Me, Mr. Davies – Hallelujah.* Bryntirion: The Evangelical Press of Wales.

Gibbard, Noel (2004). "Wales and India." *The Evangelical Magazine.* 43, 1:17-18.

Griffiths, Basil (2007). *Khasis and the Welsh Legacy.* Shillong: Akashi Book Depot.

Lloyd, Meirion (1952). *On Every High Hill.* Liverpool: Foreign Mission Office.

Morris, John Hughes (1930). *The Story of Our Foreign Mission (Presbyterian Church of Wales).* Liverpool: Hugh Evans and Sons Ltd.

Nengzakhup, S. (1999). *The Presbyterian Church of Mizoram's Amazing Mizo Missions.* Bangalore: SAIACS Press.

Robinson, Charles Henry (1915). *History of Christian Missions.* Edinburgh: T&T Clark.

APPENDICES

WELSH MISSIONARIES AND THEIR LOCATIONS

The missionaries often moved from district to district. This list gives places mentioned by my parents.

Adams, Rev. and Mrs. E.,	Silchar, Karimganj
Angell Jones	Jowai
Buckley, Miss	Shillong, then Jowai hospital
Evans, David and Muriel	Shaistaganj
Evans, Hetty,	Sylhet, Shaistaganj and other places
Evans, Laura	Cachar, Silchar, Shaistaganj
Evans, Rev. and Mrs. Sidney	Principal, Cherrapunji Theological College
Hughes, Katie	Lushai Hills
James, Miss	Silchar
Jones, Gwillym and Helen	Jowai
Jones, Hilda	Girls' High School, Shillong
Jones, Phyllis	Girls' School, Sylhet

Lewis, Leslie and Win	Maulvi Bazaar, Shangpung, Jowai
Mendus Mr.	Lushai
Morgan, Will and Phyllis	Silchar, Haflong)
Pugh Rev. and Mrs. T. E.	Principal, Government School, Shillong
Rees, Harries, Mr. and Mrs.	Haflong since 1912
Rees, Miss	Silchar
Roberts, Gordon and Mrs.	Shillong Mission Hospital
Roberts, Rev. and Mrs. J.W.	Sylhet, senior missionaries
Rowlands, Dr. Helen	Bengali scholar
Thomas, Annie	Shillong, evangelist and literacy worker
Thomas, Winnie	Habiganj, in charge of the hospital
Thomas, Huxley	Jowai, on furlough
Williams, Blodwen	Habiganj, teacher
Williams, Eirlys	Lushai Hospital
Williams, Dr. and Mrs. John	Lushai Hospital

1930 MAP OF THE MISSION FIELD

Morris (1930:102-3)

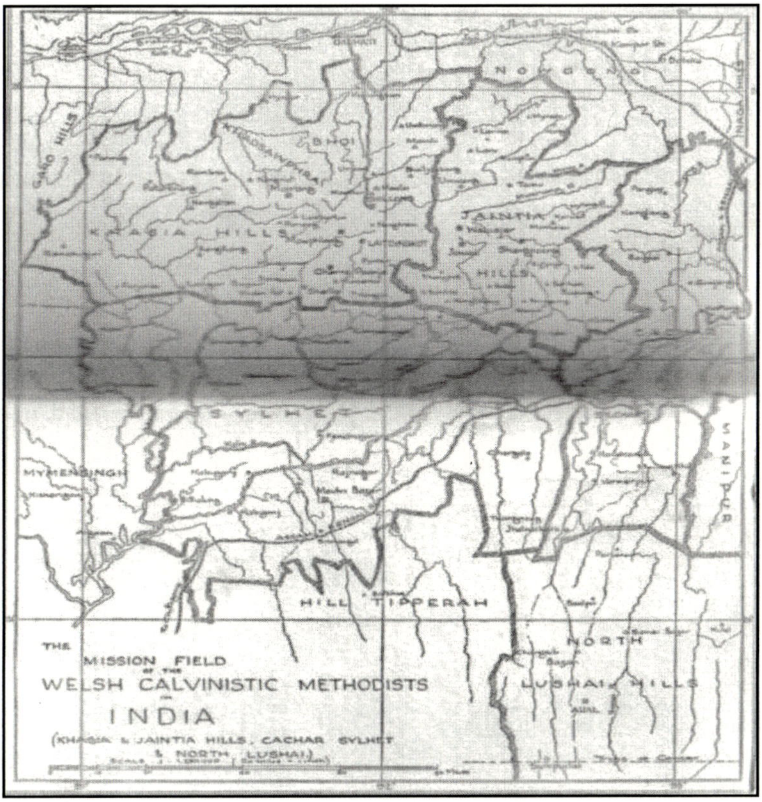